Home Safe Home

Home Safe Home:
Conquering Safety and Health
Issues at Home

Stephen Kyle Lowman
Industrial Hygiene Services, Inc.

Universal Publishers
USA • 2000

Home Safe Home:
Conquering Safety and Health Issues at Home

Universal Publishers
USA • 2000

ISBN: 1-58112-731-6

www.upublish.com/books/lowman.htm

TABLE OF CONTENTS

INTRODUCTION

Is your home safe? Most people would feel comfortable in saying their homes are safe to some degree. Have you ever taken the time to carefully consider the potential hazards that exist in your home? They are all around you. Take a brief moment and consider your surroundings. Most people do not lose sleep thinking about the associated hazards with electricity, but it exists throughout your house. If you have gas-powered appliances, how do you know that you are not being exposed to deadly carbon monoxide. I am sure that if you could examine your bed sheets under a microscope, what you would see would probably make you quite uncomfortable. The truth of the matter is that within your home, there are a vast number of chemical, physical as well as biological agents that can cause great harm to you or your family.

As a safety and health professional, I have observed that most people who work in industry are aware of plant safety rules and the consequences of breaking one of these rules. However, when they leave work to go home, oftentimes that safety awareness remains at work. Safety in the home should hold the same importance as it does in the workplace. Serious injuries or illnesses do occur at home. In fact, I am confident in saying that you probably know of an individual who has suffered a significant injury (such as a bad cut, burn, or broken bone) as a result of an accident at home. Most individuals spend a majority of their time in their home. Is it not good common sense to try to reduce the number of hazards in your home, and by doing so, reduce the likelihood for personal injury?

One of the first things people receive when they accept a new job, especially in an industrial setting, is a list of plant safety rules. I think when it comes to safety, most people view safety as being a written compilation of do's and don'ts. To an extent, this is true, but it would be impossible for a book to contain every safety rule that has ever existed. First of all, there is not a library in the world that would be large enough to contain the book, and secondly, people could spend a lifetime trying to memorize the book, and still not come close to learning what they should know.

Is there a better way to learn safety? Most certainly **YES**! People must first realize that safety is more than a list of what you can do or can not do to prevent injury, but rather is an ideology, an awareness, and a manner of living. It is impossible for me to identify every potential hazard that exists in your home, and tell you how to correct it. However, the intent of the book is aimed at creating an awareness in which you can anticipate some of the more common potential safety hazards that exist in and around your house, and aid in addressing and correcting these hazards to reduce the chance of personal injury to you and your family.

INDOOR AIR QUALITY

How good is the air quality within your home? Are you aware that poor air quality can make you sick? Most people at some point in their life have smelled an odor that made them nauseous or resulted in a headache. There are household chemicals, biological agents such as molds and fungi, and allergens such as cat dander or dust mites which can cause you to get sick at home when the gases, vapors, or the particulates (very small particles) are inhaled. Do you ever come home from work and experience a headache, feel feverish, have itchy watery eyes, a stuffy nose, or a dry throat? Do any of the other members of your family experience the same symptoms on a frequent basis? Did the symptoms appear when you moved into your home? Do the symptoms subside when you leave your home for a lengthy period? If this is the case, you may be the victim of poor indoor air quality within your home.

You may be thinking, "I don't smell anything bad in my house, so the air must be fit to breath." This notion is totally false! Why is this misconception so dangerous? There are gases encountered indoors such carbon monoxide and radon which are both colorless and odorless, but have the potential to cause great harm or even death. You can not see fungal spores or dust mites without the aid of a microscope, yet when these become airborne, they can cause serious allergic reactions. Although one may not be able to smell particular gases does not mean that they are not present.

What Are Things I Should Look for Which Lead To Poor Indoor Air Quality?

There are several questions that you should first ask yourself. Have you recently remodeled your home, or made modifications to conserve energy such as installing insulation, storm windows, or weather stripping? Does your home feel humid? Do you see evidence of moisture on the windows or on other surfaces such as the walls and ceilings? Has your home recently suffered water damage or flood damage? Is your basement damp and smell

12

musty? Is there mold or mildew growing on the walls, the ceiling, articles of clothing, books, or in the basement? Does the air seem stale or stagnant in other parts of your house? Do you have indoor pets? Have you properly maintained your air conditioning filters and cleaned any humidifiers? Do you have problems with insects such as cockroaches? If you answered "yes" to any of the above questions, the potential is there to have an indoor air quality problem.

In most cases, the causes of poor indoor air quality is two-fold. First of all, there is the source of pollution which is either biological and/or chemical in nature. The second contributor is that the materials and construction techniques utilized in modern homes reduce the amount of outside natural ventilation which enters the home. With a reduction in natural ventilation, there is an increase in the concentration of the chemical and biological pollutants within the home.

Generally, chemical pollutants are released from five sources in the home. These sources are bacteria, fungi, the off-gassing of building materials, cigarette smoke, and the incomplete combustion of a fuel source such as wood, gas, or fuel oil. To some degree, every home has chemical or biological pollutants. It is impossible to get completely rid of them. However, it is important to try to keep airborne levels of these pollutants as low as possible.

How Do I Combat An Indoor Air Quality Problem That Results from Biological Pollutants?

Have you ever walked into an old house which has been abandoned or not cleaned in a long time and noticed a strong musty odor? Chances are, the odor has a biological origin. Indoor air quality problems that result from the presence of biological organisms are very common. Biological pollutants come from organisms that are living or once were living. Examples of biological pollutants are bacterial spores, bacteria, viruses, fungi, dust mite and cockroach parts, pollen, and animal dander. Sampling for biological pollutants can be labor intensive and quite costly. Initially, you should consider another approach, and that is to control moisture levels within your home. Biological pollutants need nutrients and moisture to support biological growth. By controlling the moisture level inside the home, the amount of biological growth may also be controlled. Moisture can enter a home through the basement floor or walls. In addition, sources of moisture include bathrooms, wet appliances such as humidifiers and air conditioners, and unvented heaters. In climates which have high humidity levels, moisture levels inside homes are likely to be higher.

The most simple method of reducing moisture levels inside a home is to provide more ventilation. By opening a window at one wall and a door or another window at the opposite wall, one can provide natural cross-ventilation which might help to alleviate the problem. Ventilation can also be increased by using window fans.

Basements can be a major source of high moisture or humidity levels within a home. Even though the basement walls may not leak, porous walls can transmit moisture from the surrounding soil for days or even weeks after heavy rainfall. To check for excessive moisture in the basement, tape a small mirror (mirrored side facing the wall) against the basement wall. Check the mirror after being left overnight following a period of rain. If water droplets have formed on the mirror, the basement walls may be too porous. You should first check to see if rainwater is draining away from your house. The ground slope should slope away from foundation walls, and the downspouts from gutters should extend at least six feet away from walls. If you have water drainage problems which are leading to high humidity levels in your basement or home, consult an architect or building contractor on the best ways to improve drainage away from your house.

A leaking pipe or flooding can be other sources of high moisture levels in your home. In the case of water damage, you should clean, dry or discard any water damaged items such as carpets or furniture. Water saturated carpets or upholstery can provide a suitable medium for the rapid growth of bacteria, molds, or mildew. Allowing water damaged items to remain in your home can result in the continuous generation of musty odors and biological spores which can cause respiratory problems. Remember that by reducing moisture levels in your home, you remove a key component necessary for the growth and proliferation of biological agents.

How Do I Combat An Indoor Air Quality Problem That Results From Tobacco Smoke?

Oftentimes, cigarette smoke is a major contributor to poor indoor air quality. If you suspect that cigarette smoke is the cause of your poor indoor air quality, do not allow family members or friends to smoke inside your house. If cigarette smoking outside is not feasible alternative with others, suggest that they smoke in a room with the door closed to separate them from non-smokers. Smokeless ash trays and indoor air purifier machines may aid in reducing smoke levels inside a room with a smoker.

What Are Other Means To Combat Poor Indoor Air Quality?

A very effective means to combat poor indoor air quality is to exercise cleanliness. By using good common sense, a majority of the indoor air quality problems can be eliminated without incurring any major costs. You can keep dust levels down which can aggravate allergies by dusting your furniture, mopping, and vacuuming regularly. It is recommended that you purchase a vacuum cleaner which has been equipped with a HEPA filter as not to recirculate dust throughout your home from vacuum exhaust. Air filters in the HVAC system should be regularly cleaned or changed. Remember to change your bedsheets regularly. Flaked-off skin cells in your sheets are nutritious to dust mites. If you have indoor pets, keep them groomed to prevent excessive hair shedding in the house, and also, keep cat boxes filled with fresh kitty litter. Any fecal matter left to stand in a cat box is a very suitable growth medium for fungal agents and bacteria.

As was the case in controlling humidity levels, providing adequate ventilation can improve the air quality of a home. As the amount of fresh air that is introduced inside the home increases, the concentration of indoor air pollutants will decrease. Generally, the aforementioned methods used to increase ventilation to control humidity levels are effective in also controlling the accumulation of pollutant gases.

CARBON MONOXIDE

Carbon monoxide is a silent killer! It is a colorless, odorless gas, which can not be detected by sight or smell. Carbon monoxide is formed during the incomplete combustion of a carbonaceous fuel (i.e., fuels that contain the element carbon). Any device in your home that uses a carbonaceous fuel such as natural gas, kerosene, gasoline, charcoal, or wood is a potential source of carbon monoxide. Such devices include gas heaters, gas furnaces, gas water heaters, gas grills, gas stoves, portable generators, and wood burning stoves. Any individual who has these devices operating within their home is at risk to being exposed to carbon monoxide.

What Are the Effects of Breathing Carbon Monoxide?

Carbon monoxide illicits its toxic effect by reducing the oxygen-carrying capacity of hemoglobin within your bloodstream. Carbon monoxide has a higher affinity to bind with hemoglobin than does oxygen. As carbon monoxide binds to hemoglobin, the available sites for oxygen to bind with hemoglobin are reduced. As a result, your bloodstream will have insufficient amounts of oxygen which are needed by the other tissues in your body. People who are most susceptible to carbon monoxide are unborn babies, small children, and those with a history of heart disease or anemia.

The initial symptoms of carbon monoxide poisoning include headache, fatigue, dizziness, and nausea. It is important to note that one or more of these symptoms may occur upon exposure. However, it is also possible that none of these symptoms are knowingly experienced and that the victim simply "falls asleep" never to regain consciousness.

How Common Is Carbon Monoxide Poisoning?

According to the American Industrial Hygiene Association, approximately 5,000 people are treated every year in emergency rooms for carbon monoxide poisoning. In 1989, there were 220 deaths from carbon monoxide poisoning associated with gas-fired appliances. There were 45 carbon monoxide related deaths associated with liquid-fueled heaters, and there were 30 carbon monoxide related deaths associated with solid-fueled appliances such as charcoal grills.

How Can I Protect Myself Against Carbon Monoxide Poisoning?

The best way to protect yourself and your loved ones against carbon monoxide poisoning is to properly install and maintain fuel-burning appliances. It is also important to operate the appliances in the manner which was intended by the manufacturer. Homes which contain fuel-burning appliances should also contain carbon monoxide alarms. A carbon monoxide alarm functions by detecting an elevated level of carbon monoxide in the air which will in turn facilitate an audible alarm. The sensitivity of the carbon monoxide detector will vary among manufacturers. That is, some alarms are designed to alert individuals when very low concentrations of carbon monoxide (not immediately dangerous to life and health) are detected, while other alarms will not respond until the carbon monoxide concentration reaches a detected level which is immediately dangerous to life and health.

What Should I Do If The Carbon Monoxide Alarm Is Activated?

The first thing to do is not ignore the alarm, but respond to the alert. Immediately evacuate the house, get to a source of fresh air, and notify the fire department. If you or a member of your family is experiencing symptoms of carbon monoxide poisoning, take the affected individual to the emergency room and tell the physician that carbon monoxide poisoning is suspected. A blood test can be performed on the individual to confirm carbon monoxide poisoning. Before re-entry into your home, carbon monoxide levels have to be reduced. This can be accomplished by opening many windows and turning on exhaust fans. All fuel burning appliances should be turned off until they can be inspected by a qualified service technician to identify the source of the carbon monoxide.

RADON

Like carbon monoxide, radon is also a tasteless, odorless, and deadly gas. In addition, radon is a cancer-causing radioactive gas. Radon is estimated to be the second leading cause of lung cancer in the United States only behind cigarette smoking.

Where Does Radon Originate?

Radon comes from the radioactive decay of naturally occurring uranium in soil, rock and water and contaminates your breathing air. Radon enters in your home through cracks, concrete walls, dirt floors, floor drains, and sumps. You should also be aware that if you have a private well that supplies water to your house, radon can enter through well water. Radon can be detected any-where in the United States. Any type of building such as homes, offices, and schools are susceptible to the accumulation of radon. Being that the typical person spends a good portion of their life at home, it is imperative that exposure levels to radon be kept as low as possible.

How Do I Know If I Have A Radon Problem?

The only way to know if you have a radon problem is through testing. A test kit is inexpensive and should take only minutes of your time. Radon testing kits can be purchased at larger hardware/home improvement stores. You should purchase a kit that has passed the Environmental Protection Agency's (EPA) testing program or is state certified. These kits will usually be identified by stating "Meets EPA Requirements". If you do not perform the radon testing yourself, you should seek the services of a trained certified professional.

What Should I Do If I Have A Radon Problem?

If radon testing results indicate that there are high levels of radon in your home, you should seek the services of a certified radon mitigation specialist. Your state radiation office should have a listing of certified radon mitigation specialists in your area. There are several fairly inexpensive mitigation methods which can significantly reduce radon levels in your home. Talk to a radon mitigation specialist to determine which method is best for your situation.

What Is The Risk If I Smoke And Experience Radon Exposure?

If you are a smoker, you are synergistically increasing your chances for developing lung cancer if you are exposed to radon. If you wish to lower your chances of developing lung cancer or other health problems, reduce radon exposure and quit smoking.

FORMALDEHYDE

When most people hear the word "formaldehyde", they associate it with the embalming fluid used to preserve the deceased. However, the use of formaldehyde is widespread. It is an important chemical used in the production of other chemicals, building materials, and household products. Even though there are thousands upon thousands of different chemicals that exist, formaldehyde is one of particular interest when it comes to indoor air quality.

What Is Formaldehyde?

Formaldehyde is a volatile compound (i.e., it evaporates readily at room temperature) that is considered to be an upper respiratory tract irritant and a suspect carcinogen (i.e., cancer-causing agent). It is a colorless gas and has a strong odor. Formaldehyde can be found in a number of materials. These include the adhesive or glue used to make pressed wood products; the preservatives in some paints, coatings, and cosmetics; the coating in permanent press fabrics and draperies; the finish used to coat paper products; and in insulation materials. Formaldehyde can also be produced by burning wood, kerosene or natural gas, by internal combustion engines, or by cigarettes. Some products such as gypsum board or carpet may not contain formaldehyde when new, but may trap formaldehyde when released from other products. Then at a later time, these materials may off-gas the formaldehyde back into the air.

What Are The Effects Of Formaldehyde Exposure?

When the concentration of formaldehyde is above 0.1 parts per million, it can cause burning sensations in the eyes, nose and upper respiratory system irritation, coughing, chest tightness, wheezing, nausea, skin rashes, and allergic reactions. (A part per million can be thought of as having one green golf ball in a million white golf balls). Formaldehyde affects people in different ways. Some people are very sensitive to formaldehyde when exposed while others may not experience any symptoms when exposed to the same level.

There are individuals who will experience an allergic reaction when their skin comes in contact with solutions or permanent-press fabrics which contain formaldehyde. Such a response can result in hives, skin rashes, or an asthmatic reaction. It is hard to determine if formaldehyde is the cause of an allergic reaction, because there are other biological or chemical agents which can cause similar reactions.

If There Are So Many Chemicals That Can Cause A Similar Allergic Reaction Like Formaldehyde, When Should I Suspect Formaldehyde As The Cause Of My Problem?

Consider any major renovations that you have made to your home. Renovations might include replacing sub-flooring or existing shelving using particle-board, the installation of new cabinets, the installation of new paneling, or the reinsulation of your home with urea-formaldehyde insulation. Shortly afterwards, you begin to fill sick and experience a headache with upper respiratory irritation (flu-like symptoms). You leave your home, and the symptoms subside. However, upon your return to your home, you begin to experience the same symptoms. The cause may be formaldehyde exposure.

What Affects Formaldehyde Levels In My Home?

There are several variables which will affect formaldehyde levels such as the indoor ventilation rate, the temperature, the humidity, and the age of the material which contains formaldehyde. As the ventilation rate increases throughout your home, the concentration of formaldehyde should decrease. When the temperature or humidity becomes elevated in your home, some building materials are capable of off-gassing or releasing formaldehyde. As the temperature and humidity levels increase, more formaldehyde is released. If the temperature and humidity levels decrease, the opposite is true. Materials which off-gas formaldehyde do so more when the product is new. As the material ages, formaldehyde levels as a result of off-gassing should decrease.

If I Suspect That I Have A Formaldehyde Problem, What Should I Do?

If you suspect that you are sensitive to formaldehyde, you should consult a physician to confirm that formaldehyde is the cause. Upon confirmation, you should avoid as many formaldehyde-containing materials as you can. To decrease exposure levels, one should purchase low formaldehyde-releasing presswood products or solid wood for furniture construction, cabinet construction, or in the construction or remodeling of homes. Some products are labeled as low-emitting in regard to formaldehyde or other volatile compounds, so try to purchase these materials first. In some cases, look to use metal products instead of presswood products. Foamed-in-place insulation which contains formaldehyde should be avoided. And lastly, you should wash all durable-press fabrics before use. The above suggestions will aid in decreasing exposure to formaldehyde.

ENVIRONMENTAL TOBACCO SMOKE

It may be the case that you do not smoke. Even if you are a non-smoker, one does not have to go very far to be exposed to secondhand smoke. Although it has been the trend to phase out smoking in public places, it remains widespread. Chances are that when one goes to a rock-and-roll concert, a bar, or a bowling alley, they will leave smelling like cigarette smoke.

Environmental tobacco smoke, also referred to as second-hand smoke, is a mixture of the smoke which originates from the burning end of a cigarette, cigar, or pipe. In addition, it is considered the smoke which is exhaled from the lungs of smokers. Secondhand smoke contains more than 4,000 different chemical compounds of which 40 are known to be carcinogenic. Many of the chemical compounds in secondhand smoke are strong respiratory irritants.

The Environmental Protection Agency (EPA) estimates that approximately 3,000 lung cancer deaths are caused in nonsmokers as a result of secondhand smoke. If you have children and you smoke around them, they are at an increased risk of lower respiratory tract infections such as pneumonia and bronchitis. The EPA estimates that each year, secondhand smoke is responsible for between 150,000 and 300,000 lower respiratory tract infections in infants and children under the age of 18 months, and of these, between 7,500 and 15,000 are hospitalized. Children who are exposed to secondhand smoke are at higher risk to have reduced lung function and develop symptoms of respiratory irritation such as the production of excess phlegm with wheezing and an irritating cough.

If you have a child with asthma and they are exposed to secondhand smoke, you are most definitely jeopardizing their health. The EPA estimates that hundreds of thousands of asthmatic children have experienced an increase in the number of attacks and severity of symptoms upon exposure to secondhand smoke. If your child does not have asthma and they are exposed to secondhand smoke, they are at higher risk to develop asthma. In addition to the lungs, secondhand smoke can cause a buildup of fluid in the middle ear, which causes some children to be hospitalized. Remember that children are particularly vulnerable to the effects of secondhand smoke. Do not allow yourself or others (like baby-sitters, house-cleaners, or other hired help) to smoke around your children.

I Am Not Ready To Quit Smoking, But I Really Do Not Want To Harm My Family. What Can I Do?

Perhaps it is not the most popular answer, but the best answer is to quit smoking. By kicking the habit, you eliminate the source of what is causing the harm. However, if you or another family member must smoke, do not allow it in your home. If a family member insists on smoking indoors, increase the ventilation in that area. You can do this by opening a window and using a exhaust fan. Also, if they are smoking alone, make them close the door to reduce the smoke exposure levels to others. As stated before, smokeless ash trays or air purifying machines may aid in reducing the amount of exposure to smoke.

ASBESTOS

Do you suspect that you may have asbestos in your home? If your house was constructed prior to the 1980's, it is likely that some building materials used in the construction of your home contains asbestos. The house I lived in for 22 years contained exterior transite tiles which contained a high percentage of asbestos. In addition, the wood burning stove in our house had an asbestos-woven gasket. You should not panic, because the mere presence of asbestos containing materials in your home is not necessarily hazardous. The thing you should remember is that as long as the asbestos remains bound in the matrix material and is left undisturbed, usually there is not a problem. Problems develop when the binding materials which hold the asbestos begin to deteriorate and the asbestos fibers become airborne. If this is the case, you should become concerned. If asbestos is to be removed, make sure that you have a competent certified asbestos contractor to conduct the abatement.

What Is Asbestos?

Asbestos is a mineral fiber that was used as an insulating material because of its heat-resistant properties. It was also added to a variety of materials to add strength. There are several different kinds of asbestos fibers. Types of asbestos fibers include chrysotile, amosite, crocidolite, tremolite asbestos, anthophyllite asbestos, and actinolite asbestos. As previously stated, bound or non-friable asbestos does not usually present a health concern. However, asbestos which is contained in materials which are deteriorating, have been sawed, scraped, sanded, or otherwise mechanically disturbed can cause problems.

If I Breath Asbestos Fibers, What Are The Potential Effects?

First and foremost, breathing high concentrations of asbestos fibers can lead to an increased risk of lung cancer. As was the case with radon, if you smoke and are exposed to asbestos fibers, the risk of lung cancer is even greater. Asbestos exposure can cause mesotheoloma which is a cancer of the lining of the chest.

Another condition that can result from exposure to asbestos fibers is asbestosis. This is a condition when the lungs become scarred and filled with fibrotic tissue. People who develop asbestosis are usually exposed to asbestos over a number of years. It usually takes 20 to 30 years for asbestosis to develop after initial exposure to asbestos.

If Asbestos Is In My Home, Where Would I Find It?

There are several places where one could find asbestos, especially if the home is at least 20 years old or older. Most products that are manufactured today do not contain asbestos. The products that do contain asbestos which can become airborne are required to have a warning label. Older building materials (manufactured prior to the 1980's) that have the potential to contain asbestos are as follows:

- Insulation materials such as an asbestos blanket or asbestos paper tape surrounding steam pipes, boilers, and furnace ducts. These materials may release asbestos fibers if damaged, repaired, or removed improperly.

- Flooring materials such as vinyl, asphalt, or rubber floor tiles, the backing on vinyl sheet flooring, and the adhesives used to install the floor tile. Sanding and scraping of floor tiles and sheeting during removal can cause asbestos fibers to become airborne.

- The insulating materials found around furnaces and wood-burning stoves such as cement sheet, millboard, and paper. The door gaskets in wood-burning stoves can release asbestos fibers as the gaskets become worn.

The only way to positively identify asbestos is to perform sampling of the suspect material with subsequent analysis. Many environmental laboratories have the capability of analyzing asbestos samples. Remember that the mere presence of asbestos in a home does not necessarily mean that you are in grave danger. However, if you have a deteriorating building material in your home that you suspect may contain asbestos, it is in your best interest to have a professional sample the material. If the material does contain asbestos, and you choose to have the asbestos-containing material abated, make sure that the abatement contractor has the credentials to prove that he has been properly trained and certified. An incompetent contractor can create a greater asbestos health hazard than what previously existed.

LEAD

Occasionally when I tell a stupid joke, I will be asked the question, "Did you eat paint chips as a child? " and I will jokingly respond "why". To understand the humor in this, you would have to know that lead decreases IQ levels and delays mental development. In addition, lead can delay physical development, decrease your attention span, and increase the likelihood for the development of behavioral problems.

Does Lead Affect Everybody The Same?

The answer is no. It should be noted that children are much more vulnerable to lead poisoning when exposed to lead than full-grown adults. The reason is that fetuses, infants, and children are still undergoing bodily development, and lead is readily taken up and stored in developing bones. Thus, the uptake of lead and the overall body burden is greater in children than in adults. Children are also more apt to put their hands in their mouth than an adult increasing their likelihood for lead exposure, even though some adults are guilty of biting their nails which could be a potential pathway for lead exposure.

A simple way to reduce the amount of lead uptake in children is to provide the child with dietary foods high in calcium and iron. Foods rich in iron include eggs, red meats, and beans. Dairy products such as milk and cheese are high in calcium.

Where Could I Be Exposed To Lead?

As you may have already figured out, exposure to lead-based paint is the most significant source of lead exposure in the United States. Other ways that you can be exposed to lead is through the air that you breath, drinking water, food, and contaminated soil. Historically, lead has been used as an additive in gasoline and in solder for metal plumbing and electrical equipment.

What Are the Health Effects of Lead?

Lead affects most body systems. High levels of lead exposure can result in convulsions, coma, or even death. Lower levels of lead exposure can impact the brain, the central nervous system, blood cells, and the kidneys.

How Can I Reduce Lead Levels in My Home?

One way to minimize the potential exposure to lead is to keep your house as clean and dust free as possible. Lead can become airborne as a dust by rubbing or sanding surfaces that have been painted with lead-based paints. Always mop your floors, and wipe surfaces such as window ledges with a solution of powdered automatic dishwasher detergent. Dishwasher detergents are recommended, because of their high content of phosphate. Some multi-purpose cleaners will not remove lead in ordinary house-dust.

If your house was constructed before 1960, there is the high likelihood that any paint used on the house before that year will have a high concentration of lead. Houses built before 1978 still have the potential to contain lead-based paints. If you suspect that some of the painted surfaces in your home may contain lead-based paint, do not try to remove it yourself. Sanding or chipping such surfaces can lead to the creation of airborne lead dust which can cause widespread contamination of your home and put you and your family at risk for lead poisoning. You should consult a professional who has been trained on how to correct lead problems. You can contact your State Health Department for suggestions on how to test for lead in your house or use the services of a professional.

Be aware that on older houses, exterior paint can chip and deteriorate resulting in lead contamination on the soils surrounding the house. In addition, if you live by a major roadway which has existed for years, fumes from cars may have deposited lead in the soil due to the burning of leaded gasoline. If you walk through such areas, you may be bringing lead-contaminated soil into your house. Remember to wipe your feet before you enter into your house. If possible, pull your shoes off at the door, and then proceed to wash your hands.

If your children play outside, try to keep them in an area that is not in close proximity to the exterior of the house. Always remember to have your child wash his or her hands before you allow them to eat. Even though this sounds comical, when infants are playing outside, watch them closely to insure that they do not put dirt into their mouth.

What About Old Plumbing?

If you have old plumbing in your house, there is the possibility that you can be exposed to lead in your drinking water. For this reason, you should have your water tested for lead. Lead can leach out of the pipes or the pipe solder into the water. If you suspect you may have lead in your water, do not drink the water and try to avoid showering in it. Bottled water can be purchased at an inexpensive price. If you can not shower where there is safe water, allow the water to run for a couple of minutes before you start to fill the tub or step under the shower. The highest concentrations of lead are usually contained in the water that first comes out of the faucet. If you have an unsafe concentration of lead in your water, you should consult a qualified professional on locating the source of the lead and eliminating it.

What about Grandma's Antique China?

It is well known that some old paints used on antique china could have the potential to contain lead-based pigments. Even the glaze used on old china could contain lead. The chemical nature of some foods can cause the lead to leach out of the glaze or pigments onto the food. When you eat the food, you are exposing yourself or your family to lead. If possible, avoid eating off antique china if you are unsure whether or not it may contain glaze or paint pigments contaminated with lead. If you insist on using the China, have it tested for lead by an analytical laboratory.

HOUSEHOLD CHEMICALS AND WASTES

If you are like most average Americans, you probably could open the cabinet underneath the sink in the kitchen or bathroom and find numerous detergents and cleaners. If you have a garage or storage building, they probably contain multiple containers of old paint, partially-full gas cans, and several quarts of motor oil. Are you comfortable in saying that these items are stored safely out of the reach of children and pets? How about the storage container? Is it compatible with the chemical? How can you dispose of unwanted paints and motor fluids and protect the environment at the same time?

It is of utmost importance that we protect the health and well-being of individuals as well as that of the environment. Not only our nation, but the world as a whole has developed its highest level of environmental awareness, more so than ever before during the history of the planet. You would have had to be isolated from current news events not to have heard about the mentioning of global warming, the developing holes in the ozone layer, or the problems of disposing enormous volumes of generated waste in landfills.

I have dealt with environmental issues for several years, and have been offered many excuses as to why people do not care about environmental issues. The most common excuse mentioned is that one person can not make a difference. Totally wrong! If everyone has this attitude on the planet, the planet is doomed. Life can not sustain itself in an environment that is unsuitable to sustain life.

What Can One Person Do?

The key to solving many environmental problems begins at the individual level. To reduce the volume of trash and household chemicals for disposal, there is a very simple four-step formula you should remember. The steps are to reduce, reuse, recycle, and respond.

Packaging materials account for a large percentage of the volume of trash that is generated each year. The logical approach to reduce the volume of trash generated would be to reduce the amount of unnecessary packaging materials. When choosing between two similar products, choose the one with the less packaging material. Some hardware such as nails can be bought loose in bins instead of being packaged. Buy items unpackaged when this is an option. Consider using large quantity economical sizes for household items which are used frequently such as handsoap, pet foods, and laundry detergent. Economy-sized products usually have less packaging per unit of product.

Not only should you strive to reduce the volume of inert waste generated, but one should also strive to reduce the amount of hazardous waste generated. Try to use products of the least toxicity around the house. An example of this would be to plant marigolds near a garden to get rid of pests, instead of using insecticides with hazardous components. Your local nursery may have information or suggestions on other varieties of plants which can deter insects.

Disposing of household chemicals and paints by pouring them down a sink drain can result in an adverse environmental condition. Leachate fields can develop in the vicinity of the septic tank field lines which can impact surrounding soils and the groundwater. If you need to dispose of products which contain hazardous components, contact your local city or county government. Some communities have designated days for the pick-up of hazardous materials such as old paint, pesticides, solvents, and batteries.

Another way to reduce the amount of waste generated is to use reusable products. Examples of such practices would include using cloth diapers which can be laundered instead of disposable diapers, using rechargeable batteries instead of non-rechargeable batteries, or using real dishes which can be washed instead of disposable plates and cups.

Remember not to be wasteful. If you are at a restaurant, do not grab a fist-full of ketchup packets and napkins only to use one. Use only what you need. Being wasteful increases the amount of trash being put into our landfills.

You should try to maintain appliances and keep them in top operating condition. When an appliance does not work, what do we normally look to do? If it is older, we look to throw it away, and buy a replacement. By maintaining appliances, there will be a decrease in the replacement frequency of appliances, thus reducing junk going into the landfills.

Try to reuse bags, containers, bottles, and cans. Plastic bags from supermarkets and department stores make excellent garbage bags. Any old newspapers that you have laying around the house can be used as stuffing for gifts and packages. Brown paper bags can be used as wrapping paper for parcel packages. Old coffee cans or baby food jars make excellent containers for holding screws, nails, buttons, or other small items. However, do not reuse containers which contained a hazardous product such as motor oil or pesticides. Always dispose of such containers in accordance with applicable local, state, and federal laws.

Try to rent or borrow items that you use infrequently, and give away items that you have no use for instead of throwing them away. Oftentimes, power tools are used so infrequently that they will sit on the shelf collecting dust and rust until ultimately they are of no use. Instead of buying tools that you are only going to use once, try to borrow the tools from a neighbor or friend. In addition, if you are looking to rid yourself of usable items such as old clothes and furniture, look at donating them to a charitable organization such as Goodwill or the Red Cross instead of throwing them in the garbage. Others may find use for them, resulting in a decrease in the volume of waste items being disposed of in a landfill.

Choose recyclable products and containers and **RECYCLE THEM!** Oftentimes, by doing so, raw materials are conserved and less energy is used. In addition, by purchasing items that are packaged in a recyclable material, these materials can be recycled again at a later time.

Learn how to compost yard trimmings and food scraps. By doing so, one can reduce the volume of such material which is taken to the landfill. In addition, the compost can be used to return nutrients back to your lawn or garden. Other advantages of adding compost to soils is improved soil texture, increased ability to absorb water, suppressed weed growth, decreased erosion, and the reduced likelihood of having to add commercial additives to improve soil quality. Be forewarned that composting can attract rodents and other pests. If you are uncomfortable constructing a compost bin at your house, check with others in your neighborhood or community and ask about establishing a community compost bin.

And lastly, educate others on the need to recycle. A change for better environmental conditions on our great planet starts with you. Remember, that when we cease to exist, our children and grandchildren should have the opportunity to enjoy the beauty of the planet just as we did.

FOOD SAFETY

I once saw a cartoon of a lady who said she did her part to keep the planet green. All you had to do was look in her refrigerator. It is a sad commentary on Americans, but as a nation, we are wasteful people. Most people have more food than they can possibly eat, and oftentimes it spoils in the refrigerator.

We know the effects of eating something that has spoiled. We may get sick at our stomach, suffer from diarrhea, or vomit. Did you know that in severe cases of food poisoning, one can go into shock, collapse, and possibly die? No one likes to get sick, especially when there are preventative measures that can be taken to decrease the chances of becoming sick. Likewise, there are simple measures one can take to diminish the chances of suffering from food poisoning.

What Can I Do To Lessen The Chance Of Food Poisoning?

The first and most important thing that a person can do is wash his hands before handling food. Where your hands have been, there will your mouth be also. Always wash your vegetables and fruits before you prepare them. This will aid in removing residual pesticides that may have been sprayed on the food. Any utensils, pots, or pans used to prepare poultry should be thoroughly washed before they are used to prepare other foods. Make sure that any poultry that is prepared is completely thawed before cooking and is then well-cooked during preparation.

If a food can is bulged outward at the time you open it, do not eat its contents. In addition, use common sense when preparing foods. If it looks or smells spoiled, it is almost certainly spoiled. When canning foods at home, the pressurized cooker should be heated to 250 F for 30 minutes to sterilize food. If after canning foods, there is not a vacuum seal on the jar lid, do not eat the food. When in doubt, never taste foods that may appear to be spoiled. You can get sick from ingesting only a small amount of spoiled food.

Remember to keep food preparation surfaces wiped and cleaned, and store your foods in a clean refrigerator. Spilled liquids and out-of-date foods stored inside the refrigerator can provide a suitable growth medium for bacteria which can cause sickness. Refrigeration does not kill bacteria, but merely slows down their growth and proliferation. The colder your refrigerator, the slower the bacteria will multiply. Discard all out-of-date foods. Small children who are not able to read food containers to realize that the food is out-of-date may ingest unsafe foods.

PERSONAL HYGIENE

As an Industrial Hygienist, I have observed for years that companies will have very stringent safety procedures in some aspects, and will be lax in others. One of my favorite stories involves a Ph.D. scientist who was instructed to wear a full-face respirator equipped with mercury cartridges while working in the laboratory. This particular scientist enjoyed smoking a pipe. He enjoyed it so much that he could not wait until he was off the job or out of the laboratory until he could smoke his pipe. The scientist was so overwhelmed with the desire to smoke his pipe while working in the laboratory, that he modified his respirator in a manner that he thought would allow him to smoke his pipe while wearing the respirator. A safety professional was made aware of this very unsafe work practice, and questioned the scientist. The scientist offered the explanation that he had formed an air-tight seal around the pipe and the respirator, and no contaminant could enter around the pipe or through the mercury cartridges. The safety professional then proceeded to ask the scientist whether or not the mercury vapor could enter the hole where the pipe was filled tobacco. The scientist immediately realized that the respirator he was wearing was offering no protection against the mercury vapor.

The moral of the story is not to think that you are smarter than the manufacturers of equipment used for personal protection. Remember that oftentimes, these manufacturers have conducted extensive research on their products to make improvements for the consumer. Using protective equipment in a manner which was not intended can result in a false sense of security, leading to an overexposure to a chemical or physical agent, resulting in harm to the individual's health. Always use personal protective equipment in the manner that it was intended to be used.

There are chores conducted around the home which require the donning of personal protective equipment. Examples would include using cleaning solvents, sanding metal and wood, painting, or doing yard work. Sometimes, having the equipment on is not enough. Always inspect equipment to make sure it is good working order. Ask a welder who has ever used a welding helmet with a small crack in the lens. Even though they thought they had eye protection, I am sure that they would tell you that they learned a very painful lesson. What happened is that the lens did not adequately protect the welder against ultraviolet radiation produced when welding, resulting in overexposure. The result is the onset of a condition called photokeratoconjunctivits or as it is more commonly known, welder's flash. From personal accounts, I have heard that when you have this condition, it feels like someone has thrown sand into your eyes.

An unsafe work practice that I have observed in many workplaces and homes involves the use of tobacco products or the eating of food within the work area. I have friends who like to work on cars as a hobby. As you know, working on cars can involve the use of strong solvents to degrease parts, various paints and thinners, exposure to petroleum products such as grease and oil, and a host of other hazardous materials. They may wear protective garments and equipment when working. But many times, I have walked into a shop only to observe their chewing tobacco, bubble gum, a bag of chips, a soft drink, or lunch exposed to aerosols generated from paints, metal dusts and fumes from grinding and welding operations, and aerosol mists from blowing solvents off parts using a high pressure hose.

Consider painting a car. Does all the paint that comes out of the sprayer go onto the car? Of course not. Just look on the floor, and you will see evidence of paint overspray. And oftentimes, if a large amount of painting has occurred, evidence of paint overspray will be visible several feet away from the object that was being painted. Do you think it is healthy to eat paint? Most people would say no. But that is exactly what you are doing when you have open beverage containers, tobacco, or food in an area where an aerosol is being generated. The spraying may have stopped, but the paint aerosol may have settled onto the food, tobacco, or beverage items. When you put these items in your mouth, you can rest assured that food is not the only thing that you are eating. The solution to the problem is simple. Never eat or leave food items exposed in areas where hazardous chemicals or metals can contaminate food, and always eat your food in the kitchen, or in an area away from any hazardous materials or operations.

Always make sure you wash your hands before you eat. I heard the story of a worker who worked in a facility which utilized radioactive materials. One of his tasks involved decontaminating lead bricks which were used to shield against the radiation. This worker wore protective gloves while decontaminating the lead bricks. However, he made the terrible mistake of thinking that after the lead bricks were decontaminated, he could handle them with his bare hands. After a few months of doing this, this worker developed classic symptoms of lead poisoning. He had severe loss of muscular control and had impaired mental capacity. The most probable explanation of what happened to this worker was that he was the victim of his poor personal hygiene. He did not wash his hands after handling the lead bricks, and when he ate, he was transferring the lead contamination from his hands, to his food, and ultimately into his body. It does not take a long to wash your hands, and it will **NEVER** hurt you to do so.

Washing your hands before you eat will also lessen the likelihood of being infected by bacteria or a virus.

FIRE SAFETY

There are many things around your home which can cause or contribute to the spread of a devastating fire throughout your home. Such items include electrical appliances, fire places, stoves, barbecues, dryers, and cigarettes. Most often, the cause of fires is not directly related to these items, but can be attributed to human error or misuse of these items.

I remember when I was smaller, my mother always told me never to play with matches. Being a rebellious small child, her remarks made me even more anxious to play with them. One morning, I came across a pack of matches. I hid in the floorboard of the back seat of the car, so I could play with them without being noticed. I struck a couple and they harmlessly burned out. But on the next one struck, I accidentally dropped it on the floorboard and ignited the floorboard carpet. I was terrified! I managed to quickly extinguish the fire before it burned a large hole in the carpet or worse yet destroyed the whole car. Needless to say, I learned my lesson about playing with matches.

I have tried to instill in my young nephews that fire is dangerous, and you can get burned badly if you play with fire. Nevertheless, some people never learn, even as adults. You see signs posted at the service station that you should never smoke around the gas pumps, but I constantly observe individuals smoking while pumping gas. Oftentimes, we do unsafe things that we know we should not do, but we do them anyway. It only takes one careless act to learn a very painful or deadly lesson.

What Can I Do To Protect My Kids And Family From Getting Burned?

Always keep all matches, lighters, and flammable liquids out of the reach of children. It is inevitable that one day, most kids will want to play with fire. It is very important that you educate your children why they should not play with fire along with the associated dangers.

What About Flammable Or Combustible Household Chemicals?

Some household cleaners are in themselves flammable or are pressurized using a flammable gas. Always read the instructions on the can or container to determine the proper use of such materials. Some chemicals will ignite when used in close proximity to an ignition source such as an open flame or a source of extreme heat like an oven or stove. Never use or pour gasoline or any other flammable material in close proximity to a source of ignition. Many people do not realize that it is the gasoline vapors that are ignitable and not the bulk liquid. This means that the vapors can migrate several feet from the bulk liquid to a source of ignition and ignite. Any flammable liquids which are located around your home should be stored in safety cans, a safety cabinet, or at a minimum, in a cool area away from a source of ignition.

When chemicals are transferred from a bulk container or pump to a small container, always label the other container with the identity of its contents. I know of an elderly man who accidentally filled a kerosene heater with gasoline instead of kerosene. Luckily, he discovered his mistake before the heater was lit.

Education Is A Means Of Reducing The Likelihood Of Fires, But Sometimes They Still Occur. What Are Other Ways I Can Protect My Family Against Fires?

Smoke alarms and heat detectors can save you and your family's life. Since a few seconds can mean the difference

57

between life and death, it is imperative that you are warned when a fire starts. That is why it is so crucial that you have smoke and heat detectors installed in your home.

The location where a smoke detector is installed will greatly influence its performance. A characteristic of smoke in a fire is that it rises. For this reason, smoke detectors should not be installed near the floor, but high on a wall or on the ceiling. In addition, smoke detectors should not be installed near windows, vents, or doors where cross drafts could inhibit smoke detection. It is also important that smoke detectors be tested on a monthly basis. This includes a battery test, a test to determine if the detector will alarm, removing dust or other particulates which could interfere with smoke detection, and cleaning the batteries. There are batteries available which have an indicator on them to display how much life is left in the battery. If you do not have these type of batteries in your smoke detector, batteries can be checked with a battery tester. If you have the least amount of doubt concerning the amount of life left in the battery, go ahead and immediately replace the batteries. The price of replacement batteries is infinitesimal in comparison to the value of a loved one's life.

If you live in a house or apartment where 110 volt smoke detectors have been installed, you may want to consider having additional battery operated smoke detectors and heat detectors. The reason for this is if the power goes off, there will be no electricity to power the smoke detector.

If There Is A Fire In My Home, Would I Know What To Do?

Imagine the scene. You are sound asleep in bed, and all of a sudden in the middle of the night, the fire alarm blasts. What would you do? I can say from personal experience that this is not a fun experience. Most fires do occur during the night while people are asleep. Luckily in my case, it was just a false alarm.

The most obvious answer to the above question is to get out of the house immediately, but you should plan with your family and anticipate what to do in case of a fire. One way to buy extra time for yourself and your family during a fire is to sleep with the bedroom doors closed. Once a fire begins, it does not take long for it to spread. In addition, some materials will give off very toxic gases when burning. Toxic gases and smoke can fill an entire house within a couple of minutes.

Always have a plan on how to escape your house in the case of a fire. Practice fire drills should be held with the entire family, so everyone will be absolutely sure what to do in case of a real fire. In planning escape routes, always have two routes or ways of escape in case one of the routes becomes blocked. If you have a multi-story house, install rope ladders by upstairs windows for escape. Remember, in case of a real fire, remain calm and cautious, but act quickly. Before you open doors, always feel them with the back of your hand to see if they are warm or hot. If they are hot, do not open them. Remember that in a fire, hot gases and smoke will rise. Because of this, when escaping the fire, crawl on your hands and knees. After you escape the fire, proceed immediately to the designated meeting place so everyone in your household can be accounted for.

What About A Grease Fire?

I would guess that most people who have done any amount of cooking in their lifetime have at one time or another experienced a grease fire. The one thing you should never do in a grease fire is try to extinguish by throwing water on it. I know of cases where individuals splattered the flaming grease onto their arms or caused the fire to spread, because the water caused the flaming grease to splatter. One of the best investments a person can make in their lifetime is to purchase a fire extinguisher for the kitchen. But remember, purchase a fire extinguisher that would be compatible with a grease fire. The type of extinguisher you need to purchase would be a Class B fire extinguisher which is the type used to extinguish flammable liquids such as grease, oil, and fat. As a matter of note, a Class A fire extinguisher is used to extinguish ordinary combustibles. A Class C fire extinguisher is used to extinguish electrical fires. Fire extinguishers should be inspected periodically to determine if they are in good working order.

CHIMNEYS, FIREPLACES, AND BARBECUES

I love to eat barbecue. It is nice to live in a region where we can enjoy the outdoors while we are cooking. And as for fireplaces, I do not think there are many other things more romantic than cuddling with your honey in front of the fireplace on a cold winter's night. I appreciate chimneys because they direct the smoke from the fireplace outdoors instead of in the house.

How Can I Make My Fireplace Safer?

There are several things you can do to make fireplace use in your home safe. When you put firewood in your fireplace, always make sure you replace the safety screen. In addition, position the screen in such a manner that it will not be knocked over if a log rolls off of the fire. You should always stack logs on a burning fire in a manner as to minimize the chance of logs rolling off onto the floor. In other words, do not place too much wood on the fire at once, and stack smaller diameter logs in the grooves of the union formed by larger diameter logs placed underneath. In general, larger diameter logs should be placed on bottom when starting a fire, with smaller diameter logs placed on top. And if you ever use a fireplace and have small children, never under any circumstances leave a small child unattended in a room with a burning fire. As stated before, children are fascinated by fire, and leaving a child alone with a fire can be a recipe for disaster.

When cleaning a fireplace, be aware that coals do not have to be glowing red to cause a bad burn. All ashes removed from a fireplace should be treated as if they were "red hot". If you dump your ashes outside, make sure you do so in a place where dried wood or vegetation will not catch on fire. It is a good practice to extinguish hot ashes with water after you carry them outside.

How Can I Make My Chimney Safer?

If you use your fireplace often, you should maintain your chimney. One thing that you can do to lessen the likelihood of a housefire or woods fire is to install a spark arrestor on your chimney. They are inexpensive and can prevent a fire from starting on your roof, in your trees or bushes, or on your neighbor's property. If you live in a wooded area, remember to trim back tree limbs a minimum of 10 feet away from the chimney. The further tree limbs are away from your chimney, the better. Have your chimney cleaned on a routine basis. Solids can accumulate on the inside of a chimney and ignite, if not maintained properly.

How Can I Make My Barbecue Safer?

I have a pet peeve with portable charcoal grills. If assembled and used properly, they are relatively safe. But oftentimes, I will see individuals who think they do not need to read the assembly directions, because there is not much involved in the assembly. But what I often observe is that they will have the grill assembled in a fashion that they think is correct, will fill it with charcoal, and light it. Then when they start to place the meat or whatever they are cooking on the grill, the grill will tilt to one side because they forgot to install a bracket or other part. They will get to plundering in the box and will come across the missing part. They will then proceed to try to install the part on the grill when it is several hundred degrees hot, and they end up wondering why they did such a careless thing to get a blister or burn on their hands or fingers.

Before you light up a grill, you should always make sure that it is assembled correctly. Containers of unused lighter fluid and other flammable materials should be far away from the grill so that they will not ignite. After, you get finished using your grill, never under any circumstances should you use gasoline as a cleaning solvent to remove soot and grease. Gasoline can become impregnated in surface residual materials of the grill and cause the material to be extremely flammable. A brillo pad or steel wool can be used to remove layers of grease and soot.

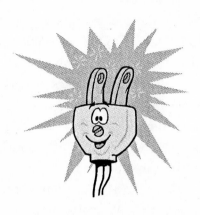

ELECTRICITY

Electricity makes life so much easier. All it takes is a power outage to cause one to realize how much electricity can be missed. Just think of the things that the mere presence of electricity allows you to enjoy such as your television, stereo, computer or video game system. You do not have to be rocket scientist to realize that there are many hazards associated with electricity. As children, we may have made the unwelcomed discovery that if we stick a metal object into a wall-plug, we would get a rude awakening in the form of a bad shock. The other major hazard associated with electricity is the potential for fire.

Using common sense can help you anticipate situations that could lead to an electrical fire. When a hazard is anticipated, act immediately to correct it. When you are not using electrical appliances, always turn them off, and if possible, unplug them. On/Off switches do fail, and the appliances can remain on that you thought were turned off. I remember several years back, I was sitting in the living room while my mother was ironing. She left the room for a brief moment, and left the iron in an upright position. While she was gone, the back of the iron started to smoke, and all of a sudden, the electrical cord caught on fire. I immediately grabbed the iron and threw it out the door into the yard. We were fortunate in that it did not result in a larger fire. Always try to purchase appliances which have been tested for safety that are listed by the Underwriter Laboratories (UL) or the Canadian Standards Association (CSA).

Never overload electrical sockets. By doing so, you are increasing your chances of having an electrical fire at that plug. Never use pennies or wires to replace a burned-out fuse. In addition, never use fuses of higher amperage than required to replaced burned-out fuses.

Remember that if you live in an old house, chances are, you have old wiring. It is recommended that you have a certified electrician to make sure the wiring meets current building codes. Over time, the insulation on a wire can deteriorate or become brittle with age and lose some of its insulatory properties. In addition, rodents such as rats can chew through the insulation on wires leaving them exposed.

Always have your heating systems cleaned, serviced, and

inspected annually. Your system should be equipped with an emergency shut-off switch. When I was going to college, I lived in an apartment which had electrical wall heaters. Over the summer, quite a bit of dust would accumulate on the inside of the heater. I was negligent in cleaning out the dust before I turned the units on during the fall. When they were turned on during the fall, I could smell the dust burning.

Most people use space heaters on occasion to provide heat. Improper use or positioning of a space heaters can cause a fire. A space heater should never be placed near flammable or combustible materials such as furniture, curtains, drapes, cleaning solvents, or gasoline. Do not ever place a heater in the path of house traffic where someone can knock it over, or fall on it resulting in a burn.

What About Electrical Shock?

Electricity causes damage to the body when the current travels through the body resulting in an irregular heart beat or arrhythmia. In addition, an electrical current can produce heat resulting in damage to organs. Our bodies are predominantly composed of water, thus they are good conductors of electricity. The skin offers resistance to the passage of current through the body. Being grounded means that the individual is sitting or standing on a good conductor of electricity. The more "grounded" an individual is, the better they will be at conducting electricity. Someone who is wearing rubber-soled shoes would not be as grounded as an individual who is barefooted. Comparatively, if both individuals were exposed to the same current, the person wearing the rubber-soled shoes would be less likely to be harmed.

There are two types of electrical current. The first type is direct current (DC). The second type is alternating current (AC). Alternating current is more dangerous than direct current, because alternating current can result in sustained muscle contractions leading to the victim's inability to release or let go of the source of the current such as an electrical wire, an antennae which has came in contact with electrical wires, or a power tool which is short-circuited to the metal casing.

Interestingly, a current as small as one-tenth of an amp, is capable of causing heart arrhythmia, and if this same amount of current passes through the brain stem, the result could be that the heart will stop beating and breathing will cease. To get an idea of the magnitude of such a current, one-tenth of an amp is about the amount of current that passes through the filament of a very low-powered light-bulb.

Many people suffer electrical shock as a result of using faulty extension cords. When using extension cords, never use cords which have damage to the insulation. Never plug up extension cords or any other electrical device with wet hands. And lastly, never remove the ground prong from an electrical cord. If you need to plug an extension cord into a wall plug without a inlet for the ground prong, purchase an adapter to go on the end of the extension cord.

There are times when unqualified people try to make repairs to electrical equipment or appliances. It is best to have a professional electrician or repairman service any appliances or electrical equipment which are in need of repair. If you plan to do the repairs yourself, **ALWAYS** make sure the power is off to the electrical appliance. Be aware that some electrical equipment such as a television contain capacitors that are still capable of shocking you, even though the television set is unplugged. Remember to wear rubber-soled shoes when working on electrical equipment. Not doing so can result in a shocking experience.

Lastly, if you have small children, purchase plug guards to prevent infants from sticking objects like keys, knives, paper clips, coins, or other metal objects into the plug. I once knew a kid growing up whose nickname was kilowatt. Guess what he did to earn that nickname? Lucky for him, he learned his lesson and survived.

What Should I Do If Someone Suffers From An Electrical Injury At My Home?

The first thing you should do is separate the victim from the source of the electricity. You should be very cautious in doing this, because if not done correctly, you can be electrocuted also. Try to pull the electric cord out of the outlet. If this can not be done, stand on a dry insulator (materials which do not readily conduct electricity) such as a thick book and push the victim away from the source using a dry broomstick. Immediately summon medical attention. If the victim is unconscious and is not breathing, initiate cardiopulmonary resuscitation (CPR).

Remember that electricity is a useful commodity, but it must be treated with the utmost respect!

COMPUTER WORKSTATION LAYOUT

We live in a computer oriented society. With the onset of the Internet, most Americans have a personal computer in their home or at least have access to one. Sometimes, it is very easy to lose track of time surfing the net, and you can spend hours at the computer station without realizing it. Some individuals may even spend hours in front of a computer at work, in addition to the time they spend in front of one at home. We have probably at some time or another have suffered from symptoms related to poor computer station layout such as eye fatigue to back pain. Proper computer workstation layout can circumvent the occurrence of home or work-related musculoskeletal disorders. Generally, the layout of the computer monitor and keyboard, the lighting and seating are important in preventing the occurrence of related musculoskeletal disorders and eye discomfort. Workstations which are shared among co-workers or family members should be easily adjustable so that the screen and keyboard can be at the proper level for different individuals. Below are a few pointers which will hopefully eliminate discomfort or related disorders from working at a computer for long periods of time.

• Maintain a neutral posture at the keyboard and mousepad. Arms should be comfortably at the sides, elbows bent at approximately 90 degrees, forearms parallel to the floor, knees slightly below the hips, and the wrists straight.

• The work station should have a large enough surface to support the keyboard, mouse, monitor and the documents.

• The top line of the screen should be just below eye level to keep the neck straight. Adjustable tables or platforms can help bring the computer screen to the proper height. Screens that tilt vertically and swivel horizontally help the worker adjust the best viewing angle.

• Monitors should be placed 18-30 inches away from the worker for viewing.

• Keyboards and monitors should be detachable so the

angle and position can be adjusted.

- Keyboard and work-surface edges should be rounded. There should be no blunt edges that can cause stress on the hands and wrists. Wrist/palm rests may be used to protect wrists and palms from hard or sharp edges and to help keep the wrists in a neutral position. However, resting wrists on a wrist/palm rest during keying can put pressure on the nerves. Wrist/palm rests should be made of soft but supporting material and should be at the same height as the front edge of the keyboard.

- Documents should be placed at the same height and distance as the computer screen. They should be easily viewed so that the individual's head is not turned to the side or tilted up or down regularly.

- To prevent glare, the monitor and keyboard should be perpendicular to windows and between (not directly under) overhead lights.

- The screen brightness and contrast should be easily adjustable.

- The screen characters should be displayed clearly with no waviness or flickering.

GUN SAFETY

In the south, it is ritualistic for a father to teach his son to hunt. My friends and I were hunting at a very young age with parental supervision. Having a gun in the house or allowing your kids to shoot a gun does not make you a inept parent. But, with the ownership of a gun comes **GREAT RESPONSIBILITY**. It is of utmost importance that parents communicate to their children that guns are meant to kill, and if they do not kill, they will maim or cause severe bodily harm. In addition, kids need to realize that misuse or improper handling of a gun can result in their death or the death of an innocent individual. Oftentimes, education and not threats, will cure the curiosity that draws a child to play with a gun.

Hunting accidents or misintentional use are not the only causes of death or injury resulting from guns. In the small town that I am from, it is not uncommon to hear of a gun discharging while someone was cleaning it and did not realize that it was still loaded. I have also heard of instances where people got shot when they got their gun out from behind the seat of their truck or vehicle and accidentally pulled the trigger or bumped it causing it to fire. I personally know of two cases where a pistol went off in a handbag at school when it was dropped on the ground. In one of the cases, a teacher was shot in the arm.

If you own a gun, there are certain precautions that you should take to insure the safety of yourself, your family members, and others. Remember to always store your gun unloaded, and store the ammunition in a separate, secure place away from the firearm. If guns are stored in a locked cabinet, keep the key in an inaccessible place to children. A trigger lock can be placed on the firearm to prevent accidental discharge. Before handling a gun, make sure that it is unloaded.

If you have children, they should be educated at an early age about the responsibilities of having guns in the house and the associated dangers. If you have very young children, it is best to keep the guns out of their sight in a secure place. Many toy guns are made to look like real guns. A child may mistake a real gun for a toy gun, point the gun at a loved one, and playfully pull the trigger not realizing what is about to happen. You should explain to your children the differences between guns shown in cartoons and video games and the damage that real guns are capable of causing.

You may not have guns in your house and may not see the need to educate your children on gun safety. However, chances are that your children will make friends with other children and may be invited into a home where guns are present. Before you allow your child to sleep over at a friends house, ask the other parents if they have guns in the house, and if they do, how they are stored. If you are uncomfortable with the gun situation at another house, have your child invite the friend to his house and explain why to your child. Your children should be taught that if they come across a gun in their home or in a friends home, they are to stop, they are not to touch the gun, they should leave the area, and tell an adult.

YARD SAFETY

Many injuries or ill-wanted health effects come from doing yard work. People get stung by bees, wasps, fire-ants
or other insects while cutting grass. They get into poison
oak and poison ivy while clearing weeds from their flower
beds. Perhaps a person stays outside to long in the hot
weather and develops a heat rash or even may suffer a
heat stroke. If you really think about it, there are a lot of
things that can happen to you while doing yard-work.

How Can I Make Yard Work Safer?

I remember growing up, when it was time to cut the grass, my mother made me wear safety glasses. I was afraid one of my friends would see me with those glasses on and refer to me as a nerd. Looking back, I appreciate her concern, and maybe because of her instruction, I still have sight in both of my eyes. The truth of the matter is that some people are not so lucky. Think about what happens when a lawnmower blade hits a rock or a stick. Most of the time, the guard on the mower will prevent the object from hitting anything other than the side of the mower. However, if you have cut grass any length of time, you would know that lawnmower guards do not stop everything. And occasionally, people get hit in the eyes by these objects moving at high velocities resulting in eye injuries or blindness. The simple way to prevent something detrimental happening to your eyes is to wear approved safety glasses. Now, manufacturers of safety glasses have developed styles that are in with the times, so you do not have to be embarrassed to wear them.

Not only should you wear glasses cutting grass, you should do the same when weed-eating. I personally know of an individual who had a piece of weed-eating line penetrate his eyeball, and another individual who is blind as a result an object hitting him in the eye while weed-eating.

Remember never to remove or alter a guard on a mower, and never remove a kill switch from a mower. Never tape or tie a kill switch on a push mower handle to prevent it from shutting off when you release the handle. Kill switches are put there for a purpose. Kill switches were developed to turn the motor off if the person let go of the handle or fell off the seat on a riding mower. Never place your hand underneath a mower with a moving blade. You will see a person with missing fingers and ask them what happened. Oftentimes, they will tell of mowing high grass, and the grass accumulated by the guard on the mower, resulting in the mower engine trying to shut off. They lifted the guard to remove the excess grass thinking that there hand would not become caught in the blade, and the next thing they know, their fingers and hand are pulled into the blade.

When using mowers, weed-eaters, or chain-saws, if you have not already suffered hearing loss, you would notice that there is high levels of noise associated with their operation. For that reason, it is recommended that you always wear some form of hearing protection whether it be ear muffs or ear plugs. Years of operating loud machinery or power tools can lead to irreversible hearing loss.

Never under any circumstances should you pour gasoline into a hot lawnmower engine. A lawnmower which has operated for only seconds can generate enough heat to ignite gasoline. You should allow several minutes (preferably at least 30) to allow the mower to cool before refilling it with gasoline. When filling a gas tank on a mower, use a funnel. If used correctly, this will prevent gasoline from spilling onto the hot engine block or the muffler and igniting. And as a matter of note, if you have gasoline at your house, store it in a labeled safety can, in a cool place, out of the reach of children.

What About Large Mowers Such As Bush-Hogs or Belly-Mounted Tractor Mowers?

I have observed times when the grass may have been too tall to cut with a small push mower, so the yard was bush-hogged instead. If you use a bush-hog, it is recommended that you wear head and eye protection. If you think that lawnmowers can launch objects, wait until you see something come flying out from underneath a bush-hog. If you know of someone who is cutting the grass with a bush-hog, you should maintain a large distance between yourself and the bush-hog.

Over the years, the yard at the home where I grew up kept expanding. I should have been an explorer, because my parents made me go with a mower where no one else had ever been before. Our yard was always full of small tree trunks and rocks ranging from pebble size to about the size of a small brick. One summer, the grass had gotten so high that it was impossible to cut it with a push mower. So dad hooked up the bush-hog to his tractor, and commenced cutting the grass. While he was bush-hogging the grass, I was walking through the living room and noticed a huge rock roughly about the size of a base-ball lying in the floor. I glanced up to notice that the rock had burst a large hole in our front wooden door. That rock probably traveled a minimum of 30 feet before it got to the door. If that was not enough, a short time later, my father's pick-up window got completely shattered while he was bush-hogging this particular area. Now I hope you realize why you should never be in close proximity to anyone who is bush-hogging. Large objects can fly out from underneath bush-hogs with high force.

What About Cutting Trees and Limbs Using a Chain-Saw?

My father is no Paul Bunyon. He should be the first to admit that cutting trees is dangerous. The direction they fall is sometimes unpredictable. Years ago, there were some pine trees that needed cutting in our front yard, because they were diseased and could fall anytime. My dad and a friend of his had secured a rope at the top of a tree, in hopes that by pulling the rope in a certain direction, the tree would fall in that same direction. Wrong! Needless to say when the tree was cut, the weight of the tree falling in one direction was far superior to all the tension that was in the rope pulled in the opposite direction. I remember playing ball some distance away and watching that large pine tree fall across the hood of our car.

Chain-saws can be a handy power tool to have around the house, but they should be handled with extreme care. As a rule, you should try to be at least twice the height of the tree away when someone is cutting down a tree. If you are using the saw, prior to use, always make sure the saw chain is taut or has enough tension so that it will not come off the guide when the saw is operating. Always inspect the chain with the saw off. If you detect any cracks or indentions, replace the chain. Never handle a chain without thick leather work gloves.

What about Landscaping?

There may come a time, when you may need to dig some depth maybe to install a sprinkler system, plant a large tree or bush, or to change the look of your property doing excavation and grading work. Before you dig, you should contact the various utility companies to locate any underground utilities. People contacted should include the power company, the gas company, and the telephone company. Serious accidents have occurred to individuals who severed buried gas or electrical lines. Severing an underground fiber optic cable may not cost you your life, but can be expensive to repair. The preventative measures taken initially can save you a lot of time, money, and preserve your well-being in the long run.

What About Heat Stress Associated With Yard Work?

During the summer, it will get hot when mowing the grass. One should be cautious not to get excessively hot, because overdoing it can lead to heat cramps, heat exhaustion or heat stroke. Heat cramps are painful muscle spasms which result from sodium depletion caused by replacement of sweat losses with water alone. Prolonged exposure to heat can result in heat exhaustion which is characterized by inadequate salt and water intake. This can lead to dehydration, sodium loss, and isotonic fluid loss with accompanying cardiovascular changes. Symptoms of heat exhaustion include headache, tiredness, nausea, and fainting. Heat stroke is a life-threatening condition characterized by the body's inability to cool itself. Symptoms include hot, dry skin, high body temperature, confusion, convulsions, coma, and death if not treated promptly.

What Should I Do If I Am Suffering From Heat Cramps?

Treatment of heat cramps consists of using salt tablets or drinking enough of a weak salt solution (0.25 level teaspoon of salt to a pint of cold water) to keep the urine pale.

What Should I Do If I Am Suffering From Heat Exhaustion?

You should drink plenty of saltwater (0.25 teaspoon of salt to a glass or water). Lay flat on your back in a cool place and raise your feet about 12 inches off the ground. Placing a stack of books underneath your feet will aid in keeping your feet elevated at the 12 inch height.

What Should I Do If I Am Suffering From Heat Stroke?

You should immediately go to a cool, shady place and remove your clothing. You should sit in an upright position and support your head and shoulders using pillows. Cover yourself with a wet sheet and keep it wet with cool water. Fan yourself with a magazine or sit in front of an electric fan until your core temperature falls below 101 F. You should seek medical attention immediately. Heat stroke can result in death!

What About Fire Ants?

I think fire ants are one of the greatest nemesis that you will find upon the face of the earth. If left alone, their mounds can take over a yard before you know it. In addition, if you ever step on the mound, you may have your shoe or sock covered with them before you know it, and their sting is very painful. It is very difficult to get them off your body and clothes without getting stung more.

No doubt I am 100% percent supportive of getting rid of fire ants. However, the methods people use to do so is what bothers me. I realize gasoline works quite well in eliminating fire ants. Two reasons why you should not pour gasoline on a fire ant mound. First of all, you introduce a source that can adversely impact soil and groundwater quality. There are other fire ant poisons that you can purchase that are more environmentally friendly. Secondly, I have witnessed people lighting the gasoline after they pour it on the mound. The gasoline can ignite violently resulting in severe bodily burns.

What About Poison Plants Such As Poison Oak, Poison Sumac, and Poison Ivy?

Contact with these plants in most individuals will result in a dermatitis or inflammation of the skin. Most people know the symptoms from exposure to such plants. Your skin may begin to itch, burn, or blister depending on your body's tolerance and duration of exposure. You must be aware that bodily contact with any portion of the plant, contact with clothing or other protective garments which previously contacted the plant, or contact with smoke originating from a burning plant can result in dermatitis.

If you come in contact with plants such as these, you should thoroughly wash the affected area, sponge with alcohol, and apply calamine lotion. You should also wash any clothing that may have come in contact with the plant. In case of a severe skin reaction, consult a physician.

What About Ticks?

Ticks are small, eight-legged parasitic creatures that attach themselves to human or animal skin and feed on the blood. If you have high grass, a wooded area, scrub brush, or anything else characteristic of a rural habitat surrounding your house, you may be particular prone to have problems with ticks. If you have to walk through such areas, always wear long pants and boots. You should examine your body afterwards to make sure a tick has not attached itself.

If a tick has attached itself on your body, it can be removed by grasping the tick as close to its mouth with tweezers. Make sure you remove the whole tick gently. Removing the tick by jerking may leave parts of the tick's mouth behind resulting in infection. All tick bites should be washed with soap and water after the tick has been removed.

As a matter of note, the prolonged bite of certain female ticks can result in a condition known as tick paralysis. I have had dogs who have suffered from this condition. The paralysis is caused by a toxin in tick saliva that affects the nerves that control movement. If you have a pet which suddenly loses function in their legs, this condition may be caused by a tick being attached in close proximity to the pet's spine. Oftentimes, if the tick(s) are removed, the condition will clear up in a matter of hours. When in doubt, always seek consultation from a veterinarian.

What About Insect Bites?

If you are bitten by an insect, you should wash the affected area with soap and water, after which a medicated ointment should be applied. Never scratch an insect bite. If you develop symptoms of a severe reaction to an insect bite (such as shortness of breath, swelling, etc.), immediately seek medical attention.

What About Wasp or Bee Stings?

Promptly remove the stinger and the attached poison bag with your fingernail or using a pair of tweezers. Use extreme caution not to squeeze the poison bag resulting in more poison being released into the wound. Apply hydrocortisone cream or a weak solution of ammonia to the wound. Depressing an ice pack on the wound can reduce swelling. If you develop a severe reaction to the sting, immediately seek medical attention.

What Should I Do If I Encounter A Snake?

A large majority of the United States has some type of poisonous snake. I spend a lot of time outdoors, and have probably seen hundreds of snakes in my lifetime, mostly of the non-poisonous variety. When I see a snake, I like to keep as much distance between me and the snake as possible. As you will see from the next two stories, I have literally been within an arm's length of two poisonous snakes. By sharing these stories, hopefully you can learn some valuable lessons that I learned.

When I was a toddler, I was playing outside during the summer and came across an object in the yard that fascinated me. Like any curious child would have done, I commenced to pick up the object and examine it. Just by chance, I grabbed it by the tail. My parents were outside with me, and upon realizing what I had done, they immediately rushed me to the hospital for an examination. If you have not already figured out what happened, I had picked up a very small rattlesnake.

About twenty-three years passed from my first close encounter with a poisonous snake to my second very close encounter. At this time in my life, I would come in from work or school and watch television until fairly late at night. When I got sleepy, I would sleep on the couch. It is a personal quark of mine, but I can not go to sleep without having a window fan operating in the same room. That particular summer night, my mother was worried about me and had stayed up to see if I got home safely. It was about midnight, and I was very tired and ready to go to sleep on the couch. I went to get my fan, but it was not upstairs. I asked my mother if she knew where it was, and she told me she had taken it downstairs into the basement to dry a mopped floor. She was kind enough to go get it and bring it upstairs to me. At the top of the staircase, I took the fan from her, sat it in front of the couch, and plugged it in. When the fan came on, I heard a pinging noise in the fan blades. They were hitting something which at the time I thought may have been the electrical cord. I immediately unplugged the fan. Upon closer inspection, what I discovered made me quite uncomfortable. The object that the fan blades were striking was a small rattlesnake. We did manage to get the snake out of the house without getting snakebit.

How did the snake get in the house to start with? Our best explanation is that my mother had brought some potted plants from the outside into the basement that night. Probably, the snake was in the bottom of one of these potted plants and later crawled into the fan. Always examine plants, boxes, or other container-like objects before you bring them into your house from the outdoors. Never leave patio and other outside doors open. Snakes and other animals can crawl into the house without you ever knowing it. Try not to accumulate old boards, rockpiles, or woodpiles in close proximity to the house. Snakes have an attraction for such. And lastly, remember to watch your children very closely when they are playing outside. It seems like children can always find trouble if left unattended.

If you are outdoors in an area that has the potential to

have a poisonous snake, you should always wear long pants and boots. If you are hiking through the woods, and there is a clear path to follow, stay on the path. Never put your hands where you can not see them like over your head if you are climbing on rocks, cliffs, or bluffs. Try to avoid areas of high grass and dense undergrowth. Never sleep on the ground. If you must move large rocks or logs, use a stick. If you come across a snake, do not agitate by poking at it with a stick, nor should you try to kill it. Slowly, calmly, and quietly move away.

By keeping the grounds surrounding your house maintained, you can lessen the likelihood for an encounter with a snake. If you cut a tree down, saw the trunk into sections, and remove the limbs and sections. Keep your grass mowed. And make an effort to keep garbage and animal feed inaccessible to rodents. Rodents which stay in the area around a house will in turn attract snakes.

If I Get A Snakebite, What Should I Do?

The first and most important thing you can do is remain calm. Do not cut into the bite and bleed the poison. Do not raise or elevate the injured limb. Doing so can cause the venom to spread. Do apply a pad or sterile dressing to the wound and try to keep the limb which was bitten as still as possible. Bandage the wound firmly, and immediately seek medical attention.

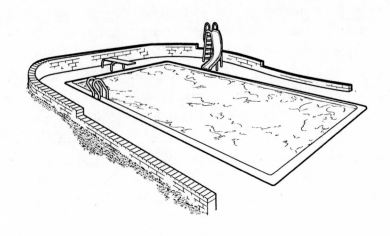

SWIMMING POOL SAFETY

What kid does not look forward to the time in late Spring when the pool cover comes off the swimming pool, so that they can go swimming. No doubt that swimming pools can be fun, but with ownership comes great responsibility. It is a grim reminder to hear on the news that a child was missing, only to be discovered drowned in a swimming pool. If you are a pool owner, you should establish a set of rules for your pool.

If you have young children, and you occasionally use a baby-sitter, they should be instructed about potential pool hazards. Baby-sitters need to know about the use of protective devices such as door alarms and latches, and should be instructed that the children should always be under constant adult supervision. If a child has played with toys near the pool side, they should always be picked up and put back in the house. Toys can attract kids out of the house near the pool.

In addition, if you throw a pool party, a child should never be left unattended near a pool. It is a good idea to appoint a person to watch the pool to make sure that no children are ever in danger of falling in the pool. If a child gets too close to the pool, an adult can grab the child before they fall into the pool or alert the child's parents.

You should realize that because children have had swimming lessons, this does not make them drown-proof. Children should always be observed when swimming by an adult, and they should never under any circumstances be allowed to enter a pool alone. "Floaties" or lifejackets are no substitute for adult supervision. As a preventative measure, it is good to know how to conduct cardiopulmonary resuscitation (CPR) if you own a pool. You can check with your local American Red Cross or American Heart Association on how to become trained in CPR.

It is important to remember that not only do you have to look out for your kids getting into the pool, but you also have to worry about your neighbors children. For this reason, a barrier should be constructed around your pool. Oftentimes, this is in the form of a wall or fence with a gate. In addition, other examples of barriers include a motorized pool cover or a gate with an attached alarm. Barriers should be of sufficient height (the taller the better) to prevent children from climbing over. Slats in fences should be spaced closely to prevent a child's head from squeezing through. When the pool is not being used, fence gates should be locked. If the gate does not have a lock, use a chain and a lock. Although, they are not totally childproof, barriers can be a deterrent to provide extra time for a parent to locate a child if they become missing.

Sometimes, the side of the house forms part of the barrier. If a house door leads out to the pool, a door alarm or a dead-bolt which can only be locked/unlocked with a key should be installed on the door.

When adding pool chemicals to your pool, do so in accordance with the instructions printed on the chemical bottle. Some types of pool chemicals react with water and liberate chlorine gas. Always mix your pool chemicals in a well-ventilated area. When you finish adding chemicals to the pool, always check the pH to insure the water is safe to enter.

Never have radios, televisions, or other electrical equipment near a pool. Electrical equipment falling into the pool can result in electrocution. It is best not to bring glass near a pool. Broken glass under water is very difficult to see, and can result in a bad cut if stepped upon.

You should always have emergency rescue equipment near a pool. This can include a life buoy or a shepherd's hook. You should always have a phone nearby. If you own an above-ground pool, remember to leave the ladder in an upright position to prevent a child from climbing in the pool without adult supervision. By following these rules, you and your family can enjoy the pool with an increased safety awareness.

SEVERE WEATHER

Being raised in the southeastern United States, I have learned that weather in this part of the country can be very unpredictable. I have seen the temperature be in the 70's during the first part of December and an ice storm devastate the area in the later part of the same month. I have been outside during the summer time underneath clear skies, and a hour later, be caught in a severe thunderstorm. But the one natural phenomenon that seems to strike the most fear and cause the most damage in this region is tornadoes.

If you have never had the opportunity to witness a tornado or the aftermath of a tornado, it is amazing the sheer power that one harnesses. I have seen massive oak trees which had survived hundreds of years of severe storms be uprooted and laying on the ground in a matter of minutes. I have seen pine trees snapped in half with the tree tops no where to be found and the trunk left in the ground. I have even observed a pick-up truck which was lifted off the ground by a tornado and was laid perpendicular across the hood of a car. I have heard reports from friends of pine needles being driven into trees and wood posts by the high winds from tornadoes.

Other forms of inclement weather which occurs in this part of the United States is severe lightning, hail, flash-flooding, ice, and snow. Most people do not think about being prepared for severe weather. The sad truth of the matter is that you constantly hear the reports of people being killed because of inclement weather. During the winter months, if there is an ice storm and the power goes off, it is not surprising to hear of a death resulting from carbon monoxide poisoning, because someone used a kerosene heater with inadequate ventilation to heat their home. Another common occurrence is to hear of people who get struck by lightning while fishing or playing golf, because they assume the storm is several miles away and poses no threat to them. Severe weather does kill. The best way that you can insure you and your family's safety in severe weather is to be prepared.

What Should I Do If There Is The Chance For Severe Weather?

If you are aware that there is the potential for severe weather, try to stay close to a television or radio. If these are inaccessible, be aware for the sounding of emergency horns in your area. If you work outdoors, make sure you are close to shelter in case a severe storm approaches.

What Should I Do If I Am Indoors And A Thunderstorm Approaches?

First and foremost, do not handle electrical equipment of any kind. Avoid using telephones if possible, and stay away from your television set. Lightning is prone to run in on the antennae, satellite, or cable connections to the television. If possible try to disconnect all television cable connections if you have prior warning of an approaching thunderstorm. However, do not attempt to disconnect cables running into your television during a thunderstorm. Also be aware that metal pipes conduct electricity. For that reason, bathtubs, showers, water faucets, and sinks should be avoided if at all possible during a thunderstorm.

What Should I Do If I Am Outdoors And A Thunderstorm Approaches?

The best option that you have is try to seek shelter inside a car or a building. If this option is not available, find an open area and squat to the ground as quickly as possible. If in a wooded area, try to find an area with short trees.

You should never stand underneath a single large tree. Remember to try to avoid bodies of water such as rivers and lakes during a thunderstorm. And lastly, try to avoid objects which may act as lightning rods such as golf clubs, fishing rods, bicycles, tractors, or metal posts.

If you should ever find yourself in an open area such as a prairie or field during a thunderstorm, and you immediately feel your hair stand up on end, this is an indication that lightning is about to strike. You should immediately drop to your knees and bend forward putting your hands on your knees. Never lay flat on the ground.

What Should I Do If A Tornado Warning Is Issued Or If I Spot One?

As stated previously, being prepared is the best defense to combat a tornado, or for that matter any form of inclement weather. **ALWAYS** have a plan as to how you will respond to a tornado warning if one is issued whether you are at work or at home. You and your family should know prior to a tornado what area of the house to proceed to in case of a tornado. If you are at home, proceed to the storm shelter if one is available. If you can not make it to the storm shelter or if you do not have one, try to go to the basement. If you have no basement, try to find an inside wall which is away from windows and lie flat against it. If you live in a multi-story house, proceed to the lowest floor. If sturdy furniture is located in a central area of the house away from windows, crawl underneath it and cover your head with your hands. The furniture can act as protection from flying glass and debris. Always keep a battery-powered radio accessible during inclement weather so you can receive up-to-the-minute updates on changing weather conditions. You should keep an emergency supply kit available complete with first aid items, a blanket, and a battery-powered flashlight.

Due to the light-weight construction of mobile homes and their large surface area, mobile homes are particularly susceptible to high winds, especially those encountered in a severe thunderstorm or tornado. If you live in a mobile home and you are forewarned about an approaching storm, you should always try to seek shelter inside a more secure building or structure.

What Should I Do If I Am Outside And A Tornado Is Approaching?

The best thing to do is try to find a ditch and lie flat in it, or seek shelter underneath a bluff or ravine if you are close to one. If you are in a car and spot a tornado, you should stop, exit the car, and lie in the ditch as before. Remaining in the car is very dangerous during a tornado. You may be able to seek shelter underneath an overpass or bridge if one is nearby.

What Should I Do If I Encounter A Flash Flood?

Try to avoid low-lying areas or wet-weather springs during periods of heavy rain. During a flood, never walk or drive through flowing water. It can be quite deceptive as to the force that the flowing water can generate, and you or your car can be swept off the roadway into deeper water. If feasible, turn off your power if you suspect that your house will be flooded. If your house is already flooded, stay away from the fuse box. Remember to stay away from powerlines during times of flooding. And lastly, be aware that utility lines such as gas lines will float when submerged underwater during flooding. As a result, be aware that gas leaks may develop. If you discover a gas leak, immediately notify the gas utility company. As a general rule, you should always be aware of how and where to turn off utilities that enter your house.

What Should I Do In Case An Ice Or Snowstorm Occurs?

In most cases, people have prior knowledge of an approaching winter storm. However, people in the south are not as prepared to deal with such storms as are people in the north and northeast where such storms occur frequently. Usually, road conditions will be worse in the south, because unlike the northern states, there are not as many pieces of road equipment available to clear snow and ice. If you are aware that a severe winter storm is approaching, be prepared. Make sure you purchase groceries before the storm and not after the storm has arrived. Many accidents occur when people try to drive after an ice storm has occurred, and they slide off the road. If you are using a kerosene heater to stay warm, make sure that the heater is far enough away from ignitable materials such as curtains, upholstered furniture, blankets, etc., to prevent the occurrence of a fire. If you have live near a wooded area, try to avoid being outside after an ice storm. Many trees and tree limbs fall as the result of the added weight of the ice. If you have elderly relatives or friends, it is a good idea to check with them to insure that they are prepared for approaching inclement weather.

LADDER SAFETY

A few years ago, I was helping a friend build his hay barn. Another friend of mine was flooring the hay loft, and had asked me to bring him some ice water. So I filled a cup with ice water and carried it up a ladder to the loft where he was working. I made it to the top of the ladder and placed the water on the loft floor. No sooner than I had placed the water on the loft floor, the ladder began to slide out from under me. I made every effort to catch the rafters, but to no avail. I fell approximately eleven feet. The sad truth to the story is that earlier in the day, the same event happened. That is, the ladder came sliding out from under me, but I was able to catch the rafters and hang on without dropping uncontrollably to the ground.

Falling from small heights can result in a serious injury, so if you are up on the ladder, it makes good sense to be as safe as possible. Always inspect a ladder before you use it. If you observe a ladder defect, repair it immediately or have it repaired. If you use a step ladder, make sure that the spreaders are fully opened and locked. When weight is applied to the ladder with the spreaders not locked properly, the ladder can twist or "walk". Before you step onto a ladder, make sure that the ladder rungs have a textured surface to prevent your foot from slipping off. Do not think about stepping on a ladder if you suspect that the base of a ladder is on a slippery surface where it can slide out from under you. If using an extension ladder, you should always have enough clearance between the wall and the ladder rung, so that the arch of the foot can be placed securely on the ladder rung. Most ladders come with a warning label not to stand above a certain rung. If you ignore the warning, there is a chance of serious injury. You may break your neck if you fall off head first.

Metal ladders conduct electricity. When using a ladder outside, always be aware of the location of power lines. Touching an aluminum ladder to a power line will certainly result in a very serious injury and probably death.

In safety, we like to learn from near misses, but we do not like it when we have near misses. I knew that the ladder had slid out from under me earlier. I should have tied-off (or secured) the ladder to an object which would have prevented it from sliding to the right, left, or out from under me. At a minimum, if that was not possible, I should have had someone steady the ladder while I was climbing and should have made sure that the ladder extended far above (at least 3 and 1/2 feet) the edge of the loft floor and made a 75 degree angle with the horizontal. So in retrospect, what did I learn? Well, first and foremost, learn from your mistakes, so as to not make the same mistake three times.

POWER TOOLS

Most every man in America has some type of power tool lying in the garage or in the closet, whether it be an electric saw, a drill, or a sander. Some of the tools are equipped with safety guards to help protect you from harm while using them. Never under any circumstances should a machine or safety guard be removed! By doing so, you are greatly increasing your chances for personal injury.

Always use tools in the manner in which they were designed to be used. People should not be involved in horseplay while using tools. To be safe using a power tool requires the complete undivided attention of the user. People should never play with tools like they are toys. A nail or staple gun should never be used for target practice. A nail expelled from a nail gun is nothing more than a flying bullet, and can kill. Keep power tools out of the reach of children. Children may mistake some power tools for toys.

Never wear loose clothing around power tools. Clothing can become entangled in moving parts and can result in serious bodily harm. Women with long hair using power tools should tuck their hair underneath a hairnet or baseball cap to prevent painful entanglements. Wear the appropriate personal protective equipment when using power tools. This includes safety glasses and protective gloves. And since water and electricity do not mix, always keep your work area as clean and dry as possible. It is well proven that improved housekeeping will decrease the likelihood of a household injury.

FIRST AID

One of the biggest frustrations I had growing up was that when I cut myself, I could have almost bled to death by the time an adhesive bandage was located. Preparation is good practice, especially when it comes to emergencies. Everyone should have a first-aid kit in their home, stocked at a minimum with the following items:

- Adhesive Bandages
- Aspirin or Tylenol
- Absorbent Gauze Bandages
- Foil Blanket
- Triangular Bandage
- Calamine Lotion
- Roll of Sterile Cotton
- Adhesive Tape

- A Flashlight With Good Batteries
- Elastic Bandages
- Round-ended Tweezers
- Safety Pins
- Snub-nosed Scissors
- Antiseptic Cream
- Antiseptic Wipes
- Hydrogen Peroxide
- Isopropyl or Rubbing Alcohol
- Ipecac Syrup

Any medications that you keep in your first aid kit or anywhere else within your home should be kept out of the reach of children. When I was younger, I thought that a particular brand of stomach medicine was the best-tasting medicine anyone could swallow. Being that I was a six-year old at the time, I figured I knew about as much about taking medicine as any adult. I had a stomach ache, so I got the bottle out of the refrigerator and instead of taking the teaspoon my mother would have normally given me, I drank half the bottle. Luckily, nothing adverse happened to me, other than I was constipated for two days. Other individuals may have not been so lucky. I definitely learned my lesson.

As parents or guardians, we have the responsibility to make certain that medications do not fall into the hands of small children. This can be accomplished simply by storing medications high on shelves out of the reach of children. If you have a medicine cabinet, you may want to consider keeping it locked. Children need to be educated about the dangers of taking medicine without adult supervision. An overdose of many medications can cause bodily injury or even death. If you have young children, the telephone number for poison control should be kept near a telephone in case of an emergency. If a child does swallow suspicious pills or liquids, immediately contact poison control. They can provide information on how to respond to the emergency.

A bottle of ipecac syrup should be kept in the medicine cabinet. The purpose of ipecac syrup is to induce vomiting in case the child does overdose on medication or drinks a hazardous substance like a household cleaner. Some liquids can be very acidic or basic. Inducing vomiting may not be the best option in that causing the liquid to be expelled from the body because further burns may occur to the gastrointestinal tract. If a child drinks a household cleaner, read the emergency directions on the back of the bottle. If you need additional information, call poison control.

Medications which are older than the expiration date should be flushed down the toilet. Out-of-date medications may lose their effectiveness, or even may result in an adverse health effect when ingested.

CUTS

Any one who does any amount of work around the house is going to experience cuts, whether it is the result of a knife slipping, stepping on a piece of broken glass, or falling and scraping your knee. Oftentimes, cuts can be prevented. Remember to keep sharp objects out of the reach of children. If a child grabs a knife or sharp object, be very careful not to snatch it from his hand. Trying to snatch a sharp object from a child can result in bad cuts to yourself or the child. Approach the child slowly in a calm manner and try to get him to lay the sharp object down.

Always wear thick leather work gloves when handling sharp metal objects such as tin or corrugated metal. If you ever break a glass object, wear thick protective gloves when handling the broken glass.

Oftentimes, good housekeeping can prevent cuts. Do not leave wooden boards with nails protruding from their surface lying on the ground. Either remove the nails from the board using a claw hammer, or hammer and bend the protruding nail ends so that they will be flush with the surface of the board. In addition, always keep nails, tacks, or sharp shards of metal off of the floor. If a person steps on such an object, the sharp object can penetrate the sole of their shoe or work boot.

If you ever have a cut, there a first aid procedures that should be followed. For a minor cut, wash your hands before attempting to treat the cut. If the cut has dirt in it, rinse it gently under lukewarm water until the wound is clean. Gently dab the wound with sterile gauze to dry it. Proceed to dress the wound with an antibacterial cream and a sterile bandage.

If you suffer a severe cut, elevate the injured body part. If a large object becomes impaled in the body or in an appendage, do not remove the object. Removing the object may only increase the severity of the bleeding. Place a sterile dressing on the wound (or around the object) and apply firm pressure to control the bleeding. If the bandage becomes saturated with blood, do not remove the dressing, but otherwise place another dressing on top of the former dressing. Removing bloody dressings can disturb blood clots which have formed and may cause the bleeding to resume. As in the case of any severe cut or instances where an impaled object is involved, immediately seek medical attention.

PHYSICAL AGENTS

A physical agent is anything such as heat, cold, or radiation capable of causing an adverse health effect such as skin dermatitis. Most Americans love to get a suntan. Think about what happens when you stay out in the sun too long without sunscreen. Overexposure to ultraviolet radiation results in skin erythema or sunburn. There are more cases of malignant melanoma or skin cancer today than there has ever been before. If you love to stay out-doors in the sun, there are precautions that you should take.

Remember, there are no two people exactly alike genetically. Just as there are differences in weight, height, and hair color, there are also differences in a person's ability to tan. It is well known that a person who is dark complected can tolerate exposure to the sun more so than a fair complected person. Regardless, it is recommended that sunscreen be utilized, because exposure to ultraviolet radiation can cause premature skin aging in all individuals. If you are a fair complected person, you should use a sunscreen with a high SPF factor. Darker complected individuals should also use sunscreen. As the case is with any radiation, there is no threshold limit where one can draw the line to what is a safe exposure value and what is an unsafe exposure value.

Another form of a physical agent is heat. You know that if your skin comes in contact with a flame, you get burned. You should know that if you get a bad electric shock, there will be parts of your body that will also get burned. Your skin is a living tissue. When the temperature rises above 120 F, damage to skin cells will occur.

How Do I Treat A Burn?

For a minor burn, the first thing you should do is immerse the burned area immediately in cold, running water, or apply a cold compress using a clean towel or handkerchief to the affected area until the pain diminishes. Any jewelry in the affected area should be removed before swelling begins. After application of the cold compress or the cool water, the affected area should be dressed with a clean, sterile, non-fluffy bandage.

For a major burn, if the person is on fire, immediately extinguish the fire with water, or cover the person in a blanket and smother the flames. Do not remove any clothing that is stuck to the wound, but cover exposed areas with a clean, dry, non-fluffy cloth to aid in preventing infection. The material should be secured with a bandage. Be very careful not to use an adhesive bandage on skin which has been burned. Removal of those bandages can be very painful to the victim, and plus, the adhesive bandage can cause additional damage to the burned area.

Remember that you are not cooking, so do not apply butter, oil, or grease to a burn. Do not apply lotions or creams. Do not prick resultant blisters with a pin. Individuals with severe burns should seek immediate medical attention.

SHOCK

Sometimes, shock is the body's physiological response to a severe illness or injury. Shock can be defined as the reduction of blood flow throughout the body tissues, which left untreated, can result in collapse, coma, or death. Shock can be the result of a severe burn, persistent vomiting or diarrhea, a heart attack, a blockage of blood flow to the lungs, inflammation of the abdominal cavity, spinal injury, and some types of poisoning. Symptoms of shock include rapid, shallow breathing, a rapid pulse, cold and clammy skin, dizziness, weakness, or fainting.

If the shock is the result of a severe cut, the bleeding needs to be stopped. To treat shock, maintain an open airway. Never should a victim be given food or drink when they are in shock. The victims legs should be raised about 12 inches off of the floor so that blood flows from the legs back to the trunk of the body. The victim should lie flat on their back, tight clothing should be loosened, and a blanket should be wrapped around them to minimize heat loss. Shock is life threatening, therefore, medical attention should be sought immediately.

PET SAFETY

I once knew an individual (we will call him Joe Average to protect his anonymity) who was very haphazard about how he stored materials and chemicals that were used around his house and farm. I constantly warned Joe that he needed to store his chemicals on shelves or in cabinets which would be inaccessible to children or his pets. Unfortunately, Joe learned a hard lesson.

Joe had two of the most playful dogs that you would ever see. One morning while visiting Joe, another friend came running into the house and said one of Joe's dogs was dying. I ran out the door, and found Joe's dog lying in the grass having convulsions. We immediately rushed the dog to the veterinarian, but it died by the time we got her there. We did not have a clue as to what caused her to die so suddenly. In the meantime, a construction crew had arrived at Joe's house to build an addition onto his barn. When we arrived back at the house, one of the worker's came running and said there was something wrong with Joe's other dog. We discovered that the other dog was likewise having convulsions. We rushed his other dog to the veterinarian's office, and as before, the dog died.

We left the veterinarian's office very bewildered as to what had caused Joe's dogs to die so suddenly. When we got back to the house, we discovered the culprit. Joe had a problem with a large number of flies inside his barn. So earlier that morning, some fly-poison had been placed in trays along the ground. As we say in the safety profession, never assume something will not happen, because the things you least expect to happen usually will happen and result in the most damage. Joe stated that his former employer had used fly bait for years and that his dogs never had disturbed it. Unfortunately, Joe's dogs had ingested a small amount of the fly bait and died.

Why share such a terrible and sad story? It is because I do not want you to make the same mistake with your pets. As bad as the events that occurred that day were, it could have been worse. Even though I was terribly distraught to see Joe lose his pets in such a gruesome manner, I am reminded that it could have been the loss of life of a small child.

Remember that dogs and small children like to put things in their mouth. Move bags of insecticides, fertilizers, automotive products, and household chemicals to a safe, secure location out of their reach.

What Are Other Ways I Can Keep My Pet Safe?

If you live in an area which has a large tick and flea population, make sure you provide your pet with protection. Put yourself in your pets place. Would you like to be covered from head to toe with ticks and fleas? Of course not! You would not like it and neither does your pet. Check with your veterinarian about which flea and tick repellents are most compatible with the size and breed of your pet. Also, take your pets to the veterinarian to receive immunizations and medications to protect them against rabies and heart worms.

Always provide your pet with plenty of food, water, and shelter. Pets need water every bit as much as humans. Pets can be a prone to problems of heat stress, so it is of vast importance that they be furnished with plenty of water to drink. Remember to change your pet's water and food daily. There are many places in the United States which are subject to very frigid temperatures during the winter, and within those areas, is a large pet population. If the temperature outside drops below freezing, make sure your pet has a warm place to go to stay out of the elements such as a doghouse, basement, or barn. If you feel that the temperature is going to drop to a level which could harm or kill your pet, bring them indoors.

And lastly, if you live in an area that is heavily congested with traffic, keep your pet inside a fenced area or on a leash to prevent them from getting hit by a car. Some towns and cities have mandatory ordinances that requires your pet to be on a leash if the pet is not in the house or within a fenced area. If your pets are kept on a leash, make sure that they will have access to food, water, shade, and shelter from rain and other inclement weather.

CONCLUSION

Growing up, I have had my share of close calls with accidents around the house. I hope the stories I have shared with you as well as the safety tips will prove useful in protecting you and your family from harm's way. As stated in the Introduction, it would be impossible to discuss every potential safety hazard that exists in your home. Perhaps at this moment, you can think of safety-related areas which were omitted. If this is the case, you have taken the first step in becoming a more safety-conscious individual, because you are thinking about safety as it relates to hazards around your home.

If you recognize a safety hazard, do whatever you have to do to control or correct it immediately. You need to "nip it in the bud!" By doing so, you can eliminate unnecessary pain and suffering to you or your family, resulting in improved quality of life.

Practice with your family emergency drills as it pertains to fires and inclement weather. Take a CPR and a first aid class. You will never know when such knowledge may save a loved one's life. Teach your children to dial 911 in case of an emergency. Simply stated, be prepared for all emergencies. An ounce of prevention is worth a pound of cure! Be safe!

REFERENCES

1. The United States Environmental Protection Agency
    and The United States Consumer Product Safety
    Commission: The Inside Story; A Guide To Indoor
    Air Quality (EPA 402-K-93-007). Washington, D. C.:
    Office of Air and Radiation, April 1995.

2. The United States Environmental Protection Agency,
    The United States Consumer Product Safety Com-
    mission, and The American Lung Association: What
    You Should Know About Combustion Appliances and
    Indoor Air Pollution. Washington, D. C.

3. The United States Environmental Protection Agency:
    Protect Your Family and Yourself from Carbon Mon-
    oxide Poisoning (EPA 402-F-96-005). Indoor Envi-
    ronments Division (6607J), Office of Air and Radia-
    tion, October 1996.

4. The American Industrial Hygiene Association: Car-
    bon Monoxide - The Silent, Cold Weather Killer.
    Fairfax, Virginia.

5. The United States Environmental Protection Agency, The United States Department of Health and Human Services; and The United States Public Health Service: A Citizen's Guide To Radon (Second Edition); The Guide To Protecting Yourself and Your Family From Radon (402-K92-001). Washington, D. C.: Indoor Air And Radiation (6604J), September 1994.

6. The United States Consumer Product Safety Commission: An Update On Formaldehyde. Washington, D. C.: October 1990.

7. The United States Environmental Protection Agency: Secondhand Smoke; What You Can Do About Secondhand Smoke As Parents, Decisionmakers, and Building Occupants (402-F-93-004). Washington, D. C.: Air And Radiation (6203J), July 1993.

8. The American Lung Association, The United States Consumer Product Safety Commission, and The United States Environmental Protection Agency: Asbestos In Your Home. Washington, D. C.: September 1990.

9. The United States Environmental Protection Agency: The Consumer's Handbook for Reducing Solid Waste (EPA 530-K-92-003). Washington, D. C.: August 1992.

10. Cote, Arthur E. and Jim L. Linville. The National Fire Protection Association: The Fire Protection Handbook. Quincy, Massachusetts: 1991. pp. 4-35 - 4-41.

11. Cote, Arthur E. and Jim L. Linville. The National Fire Protection Association: The Fire Protection Handbook. Quincy, Massachusetts: 1991. pp. 2-74 - 2-87.

12. The National Institute of Occupational Safety and Health: Elements of Ergonomics Programs; A Primer Based On Workplace Evaluations of Musculoskeletal Disorders (DHHS Publication No. 97-117). Cincinnati, Ohio: March 1997.

13. Thunderstorms & Lightning - Federal Emergency Management Agency (FEMA).

14. Tornadoes - University of Florida (Fact Sheet DH 22). Gainesville, Florida: June 1993.

15. Brauer, Roger L.: Safety and Health For Engineers. New York: Van Nostrand Reinhold, 1994. pp. 126-127.

16. Clayman, Charles B., M. D.: The American Medical Encyclopedia, Volume I, A - H. New York: Random House, 1989. pp. 456-457.

17. Clayman, Charles B., M. D.: The American Medical Encyclopedia, Volume I, A - H. New York: Random House, 1989. pp. 179.

18. Clayman, Charles B., M. D.: The American Medical Encyclopedia, Volume I, A - H. New York: Random House, 1989. pp. 219-221.

19. Clayman, Charles B., M. D.: The American Medical Encyclopedia, Volume II, I - Z. New York: Random House, 1989. pp. 901-902.